Beyond
Boardwalk
and
Park Place

Beyond Boardwalk and Park Place

The Unauthorized Guide to
Making Monopoly® Fun Again

Noel Gunther and
Richard Hutton

Illustrations by Susan Kim

BANTAM BOOKS
TORONTO · NEW YORK · LONDON · SYDNEY · AUCKLAND

BEYOND BOARDWALK AND PARK PLACE
A Bantam Book / December 1986

Monopoly® is a registered trademark of Parker Brothers for its board game equipment. This book is neither sponsored nor authorized by Parker Brothers.

Illustrations by Susan Kim.

Library of Congress Cataloging-in-Publication Data

Gunther, Noel.
  Beyond Boardwalk and Park Place.

  1. Monopoly (Game)   I. Hutton, Richard, 1949-
II. Title.
GV1469.M65G86   1986   794.2   86-47572
ISBN 0-553-34341-6

Published simultaneously in the United States and Canada

PRINTED IN THE UNITED STATES OF AMERICA
S   0 9 8 7 6 5 4 3 2 1

To our brothers,
Edward and Ron Hutton
and Marc and Andy Gunther,
the toughest competitors we know

Acknowledgments

Even a short book takes a lot of help. We would like to thank Dave Balton, Andy Gunther, Ron Kutak, and Matt Slepin for diving into Beyond Boardwalk with verve and enthusiasm and helping to refine our rules. Professors Ralph Anspach and Irvin Hentzel shared with us their encyclopedic knowledge of Monopoly® and related games. Marc Gunther, Marina Jackson, and Irene Weinstock read the manuscript at various stages, and they are responsible for numerous improvements in the book. Peter Guzzardi, our editor, liked the idea off the bat and stood behind us all the way. Bill Perry graciously allowed us to work on the book at the office of Dow, Lohnes & Albertson. Peter O'Brien, Spencer Sherman, and David Wittenstein gave us good humor and sound advice. Corinne Antley, as always, was a perceptive critic and a supportive friend. We are especially grateful to Susan Kim, who provided an editor's eye, a tycoon's touch, and the illustrations that grace this book.

We are filled with admiration for the game of Monopoly® itself. Its fifty years at the top of the heap attest to its greatness.

Contents

PART 3. TRAINING AND ETIQUETTE

APPENDICES

Beyond
Boardwalk
and
Park Place

Introduction

"We abide by the Golden Rule. The one with the gold, rules."

—Edward Bennett Williams

Remember Monopoly®? You loved it when you were ten years old. You finally found a game you could beat your parents at. And you felt pretty shrewd doing it, too—you were buying property, building houses, controlling a vast fortune in play money. It was heady stuff.

Then you turned eleven and you started to get bored with the game. Every time someone landed on a property, he bought it. Everything depended on the roll of the dice. The game lasted too long. Then your eight-year-old sister beat you, and you *knew* it was all just a matter of luck. So you put the game in the closet, somewhere between Candy Land® and Electric Football®. And it's been there, gathering dust, ever since.

That's how it went with us, until one day last winter. We'd given up on Trivial Pursuit™, Boggle® was a bore, and it was too cold to go outside. In desperation we pulled out the Monopoly® set.

After a few rolls we remembered why we'd stopped playing the game in the first place. So we started tinkering with the rules. Why not put more skill into the game? Why not speed it up? Why not make every purchase a risk, every roll of the dice important—for everybody?

That day, we began to develop our own version of the

game. We started with the idea of auctioning the properties; then we experimented with dozens of other rules. After several months, and several hundred games, we had finally created Beyond Boardwalk and Park Place, the modern, fast-paced version of Monopoly®.

Beyond Boardwalk and Park Place takes this Depression-era game and streamlines it for the 1980s. You don't need any fancy equipment to play; just use the standard Monopoly® set, plus the "Go cards" that appear on pages 101-106 of this book.

Part One

Getting Started

Chapter 1

From Monopoly® to Beyond Boardwalk

"Monopoly® evokes a unique emotion, the surge of thrill you get when you know you've wiped out a friend."

—Shelley Berman

A legend has grown up about the origins of Monopoly®. It goes like this: Unemployed salesman has time on his hands during the Depression; dreams of his days on the beach at Atlantic City; invents a new game about buying up all the property in Atlantic City; sells the idea to Parker Brothers and becomes rich. It's a touching story, but the truth is more complicated.

Just as baseball was derived from rounders and Oreos from Hydrox, Monopoly® was based on something called The Landlord's Game. But while Monopoly® glorifies the pursuit of wealth, the original game had more idealistic origins.

The Landlord's Game was invented in 1904 by Elizabeth Magie Phillips of Washington, D.C. Mrs. Phillips was a follower of Henry George, an economist who believed that all taxes should be replaced by a single tax on land. The original board reflected Mrs. Phillips's irreverent attitude toward business. The squares included "Lord Blueblood's Estate" and "The Soakum Lighting Co."

During the 1920s, The Landlord's Game and early versions of Monopoly® were played on college campuses throughout the Northeast. The game was passed around informally—

neither the board nor the rules were standardized, and players used the names of streets from their hometowns. At one point a young visionary offered the game to Milton Bradley, but the company rejected it.

Monopoly® was still largely unknown when Charles Todd began playing an Atlantic City version in the early 1930s. One day Todd ran into an old high school classmate, Esther Darrow. He hadn't seen Mrs. Darrow for twenty years, but he invited her to his house to play Monopoly®.

Mrs. Darrow's husband, Charles, was fascinated by the game. Shortly after that evening with the Todds, he decided to make his own set. He built the first houses and hotels by hand, from scraps of wooden molding discarded by a local lumberyard. He typed the title cards on pieces of cardboard. He painted the board on the oilcloth that covered his kitchen table.

Darrow played Monopoly® with his friends and then started making sets for them. After about a year he decided to market the game more formally. Soon the Philadelphia department stores were ordering more sets than Darrow could make himself.

In 1934, Darrow offered the game to Parker Brothers, but he ran into difficulties. Parker Brothers had a set of guidelines for family games. A game should last no more than forty-five minutes. It should have a defined end point, such as square 100 in Chutes and Ladders®. Parker Brothers also thought that games should be easily understandable and free of technical terms like *mortgage* and *title deed*.

After several weeks of testing, Parker Brothers rejected Monopoly®. The company told Darrow that his game contained "fifty-two fundamental errors" and would never catch on with the public. But Darrow persisted; he continued producing sets, and people continued to buy. Several months later, Robert Barton, president of Parker Brothers, happened to pick up a copy of the game at F.A.O. Schwarz in New York. Barton loved it; he wrote to Darrow the next day. In March 1935, Parker Brothers bought the game.

Since then, Monopoly® has been remarkably successful.

Parker Brothers has sold more than 90 million sets, and the game has been translated into nineteen languages. Monopoly® has been played in a hotel elevator (for 148 consecutive hours), on a dorm room ceiling (defying gravity), and even underwater. Parker Brothers now prints more money every year than the United States Mint and builds more houses than the entire U.S. real estate industry.*

Monopoly®, therefore, is one of the great success stories in the history of board games. So why did we develop our own rules? Well, there may not be "fifty-two fundamental errors" in Monopoly®, but the game has problems in the fast-paced eighties:

• *It takes too long.* According to Parker Brothers, the record for the longest Monopoly® game is 1,416 hours (fifty-nine days). As far as we know, the record for the shortest game is only ten minutes less than that. Some games seem to last fifty-nine years.

• *There's too much luck.* Like Risk® and Backgammon, Monopoly® depends too much on the roll of the dice. Its strategy can be mastered in twenty minutes and summarized in five words: Buy Everything You Land On. As a result, the game is not very challenging.

• *There's too much dead time.* There are only two ways to keep busy during other players' turns. If you're honest, you can pull out $2 in Monopoly® money and ask your kids to get you a snack. If you're dishonest, you can steal from the Bank when nobody's looking. Most of the time that's easy, because everyone has fallen asleep.

---

*Darrow, meanwhile, marketed one more game, Bulls and Bears, which turned out to be a dog. At age forty-six he retired on his Monopoly® royalties and became a gentleman farmer. A plaque at the corner of Boardwalk and Park Place in Atlantic City memorializes him as "the inventor of the Game of Monopoly®."

We created Beyond Boardwalk to put more skill into the game; to make it faster, livelier, and more competitive. Beyond Boardwalk makes Monopoly® fun again, for adults as well as children.

Chapter 2

How to Play the Beyond Boardwalk Way

"Money is the seed of money, and the first guinea is sometimes more difficult to acquire than the second million."

—Jean Jacques Rousseau

The following rules enhance the rules that come with each Monopoly® set.* They are easy to follow and easy to implement. Real estate tycoon Donald Trump spends all his time playing with ideas like these. In Beyond Boardwalk, beginning with a mere $1,500, you can put all of Trump's tricks to work.

The Auction Block

Rule 1. *When you land on a property, you can buy it outright for double the list price. If you don't want to buy at that price, the property is auctioned off.*

The biggest problem with Monopoly® is its predictability. You land on St. Charles Place, you buy it. You land on Boardwalk, you buy it. Properties are so inexpensive that the roll of

---

*For the sake of convenience, we've included a complete set of rules in Appendix B. The Appendix can be used as a reference if questions come up during the course of a game.

the dice is the only factor that determines who gets what. The building of monopolies—the key to the game—is therefore ruled almost totally by chance.

We've changed all that. When you land on a property, you still have the right to buy it—but at double its listed price. That means $400 for New York Avenue, $800 for Boardwalk. Since you begin the game with only $1,500, you can't afford to buy everything you land on. If you did, you'd go broke in four turns.

The result is that virtually every property goes up for auction. The minimum bid is half the list price plus $10—that is, $110 for New York Avenue, $210 for Boardwalk. After the opening bid, the auction continues, each player bidding in turn. The auction ends when one player has made a bid and the other players pass. If everybody passes on the opening round of bidding, the property remains unsold. A new auction is held the next time someone lands on the property.

This simple change means that almost every roll of the dice pits the players against one another in a contest of bidding, bluffing, and skill.

The End of the Mortgage

Rule 2. *There are no mortgages. You can sell a property back to the Bank at any time, for half its list price.*

In Monopoly®, a player in a pinch can raise money by mortgaging a property—flipping the deed over and collecting half its list price. He continues to own the property, but as long as it's mortgaged, it's useless. The property pays no rent, and the owner can keep it out of circulation forever. By mortgaging a property, you create an instant slum.

In Beyond Boardwalk, you use it or lose it. You can still

raise the same amount of cash by flipping a deed—only now you have to flip it all the way back to the Bank. This means that the property becomes available again. The next time someone lands on it, the bidding begins just as if the property had never been owned. The deeds stay in circulation, and players pay a stiff penalty for foolish purchases.

Return of the Rail Barons

Rule 3. *Water Works and Electric Company are treated like railroads, so there are now six railroads in the game. If you own all six, you collect $400 each time someone lands on any of your railroads.*

What can you say about Electric Company and Water Works? In the real world they give you brownouts and murky water. In Monopoly® they are the two dullest properties on the board. They can never be developed with houses or hotels. Even if you own both utilities, you earn only ten times the roll of the dice. That means the maximum rent is only $120 ($10 times twelve). We found, after a few games, that the properties weren't selling for even the minimum bid; they were just more dead space. So . . . we converted them into railroads.

Now there are six railroads in the game instead of four, and the maximum rent payment is $400, instead of $200. This makes the railroads far more powerful. Transportation charges are as follows:

If you own one railroad	$ 25
If you own two railroads	$ 50
If you own three railroads	$100
If you own four railroads	$200
If you own five railroads	$300
If you own six railroads	$400

Four hundred dollars is serious money. When you face this kind of rent, you get very nervous about taking a ride on the Reading.

Since Water Works and Electric Company count as railroads, their "list price" is now $200 (instead of $150), the minimum bid is $110 (as always, half the "list price" plus $10) and the resale price (if you sell back to the Bank) is half the list price, or $100.

If you draw the Chance card that says "Advance token to the nearest Railroad," you move your token to one of the four original railroads: Reading, Pennsylvania, B & O, or Short Line. If you draw the card that says "Advance token to nearest utility," you advance to either Electric Company or Water Works, and pay the owner twice the rent to which he or she is normally entitled in Beyond Boardwalk.

Bankruptcy

Rule 4. *A player who is not in debt may voluntarily declare bankruptcy. He receives $800, plus the dark-purple monopoly (Mediterranean Avenue and Baltic Avenue).*

Bankruptcy in Monopoly® means death. You're out of the game, on your way to the refrigerator to take out your frustrations on leftover roast beef while the others are still enjoying themselves.

In real life, though, bankruptcy can be a blessing—just ask Penn Central or Braniff. You make some mistakes, wind up hopelessly in debt—and then, with a few strokes of the pen and minimal embarrassment, those nasty creditors disappear. You're back on your feet, poorer, hopefully wiser, and with a clean slate.

That's how it works in Beyond Boardwalk too. A player on the brink of extinction can *voluntarily* declare bankruptcy before a magnate picks him off. He surrenders his assets to the Bank and is given a new lease on life: the low-rent monopoly of Mediterranean and Baltic, plus $800 in cash. That's enough money to build hotels on both properties and still have $300 left over. It's usually not enough to win the game, but anything can happen. . . .

In one game, our friend Susan landed on Indiana Avenue—just after another player had built a hotel there. Susan added up her assets and found herself with $1,055—just five dollars more than the hotel bill. She had to pay the rent in full, since a player who does not pay his debts loses the game. But after shelling out the $1,050, Susan voluntarily declared bankruptcy and immediately built a hotel on Baltic Avenue. She was promptly rewarded when the magnate who almost bankrupted her came visiting on the next turn and had to fork over $450. Susan now had $1,000—enough to buy some additional property. She didn't win the game, but she hung around long enough to see two opponents go broke.

If you own Mediterranean or Baltic, and someone else declares bankruptcy, don't worry. The Bank will pay you $120 for each property—double the list price. The Bank will also give you $50 for each house you have built on either property.

Bankruptcy can only be used once in each game. After one player declares bankruptcy, neither he nor any other player can declare bankruptcy again in that game. Even among paupers, it pays to be first.

Go Cards

Rule 5. *Every time you land on Go, you draw a Go card.*

In Monopoly®, the Go square is just more dead space. It's great when you collect $200, but when your opponents land there, all you can do is sit back and watch.

In Beyond Boardwalk, we've given Go some gusto. When you land on Go, you still collect $200; but you also draw a Go card. The *Go* cards allow you to tweak the other players—or allow them to tweak you.*

Here's what the cards say:

1. You've been elected sheriff. Send another player to Jail.
2. The railroads announce a special youth fare. Deduct 50 percent from the rent the next time you land on someone else's railroad.
3. You win a "night on the house." The next time you land on anyone else's property, you are excused from paying rent.
4. You marry one of your tenants. Collect $25 from each player as a wedding gift.
5. Your brother-in-law becomes president of the Bank. The Bank will contribute $100 to your final bid in the next auction.
6. The railroads run late—again. If you own any railroads, pay each player $50 as a refund for poor service.
7. Your renovations pay off. Collect $50 in extra rent from the next player who lands on any of your properties.
8. You decide to take up golf. Pay each player $25 for private lessons.
9. Advance to Free Parking and collect the jackpot, if any. Give each player $50 as a tip for parking your car.
10. You hold a party to curry favor with community leaders. Pay $25 for the curry.
11. The city condemns one of your houses. Sell one house back to the Bank at half the price you paid for it.

---

*A complete set of *Go* cards appears on pages 101-106.

12. Your friends honor you as "Tycoon of the Year." Collect $50 from each player.

Singles Barred

Rule 6.   *Do Not Use the $1 Bills.*

To speed up the game, we have rounded off all rents to the next highest $5 and thrown out the $1 bills. This means the rent for Oriental Avenue (list rent $6) is $10; for Kentucky (list rent $18), it is $20. If you own the light-blue monopoly (Oriental, Vermont, and Connecticut) and would normally collect double rent, the rent for landing on Oriental is $15 (two times $6 equals $12, which is rounded up to $15). Why waste time making change when you could be outbidding or outsmarting your opponents?

During an auction, each bid must raise the previous bid by at least $5. If you bid $200, your opponent's next bid must be at least $205.

Crime Doesn't Pay

Rule 7.   *If you are in Jail, you cannot bid on property, you cannot build houses, and you collect only half the normal rent if somebody lands on your property.*

In Monopoly®, Jail is a haven, especially late in the game. White-collar criminals can relax in Jail for three straight turns, happily collecting rent while enjoying country-club surroundings.

We've cracked down on criminals by making it impossible for them to conduct business from their Jail cells. In Beyond Boardwalk, criminals usually repent immediately—they pay their $50 fine and get back in the game.

Return of Free Enterprise ·

Rule 8.   *If you own a monopoly, you can build houses on any property. You do not have to build evenly.*

Monopoly® demands even building—all properties within a monopoly have to have one house before you can build a second. In Beyond Boardwalk, you live and die by your wits. Our rules let you build unevenly. If you want to take a chance and put a hotel on States Avenue, leaving St. Charles and Virginia naked, it's your funeral.

Free Parking, Free Lunch

Rule 9.   *Taxes and house assessments are paid into a kitty. If you land on Free Parking, you collect the kitty.*

Parker Brothers is puritanical about Free Parking: "A player landing on this space does not receive any money, property or reward of any kind. This is just a 'free' resting place."
Lighten up, guys—it's just a game. In Beyond Boardwalk, all taxes and house assessments are paid into the kitty, and anyone who lands on Free Parking cleans up. We like this rule. If we land on Free Parking, we consider it a matter of skill. On the other hand, if one of us loses to a novice, our excuses begin with the lucky roll that gave him a nest egg.

When To Build

Rule 10.   *You can buy houses only immediately before your turn.*

Building Unevenly

Free Parking

Do you have the urge to build? Monopoly® lets you buy houses at any time. Beyond Boardwalk forces you to take a risk. Suppose, for example, that it's your turn and you're near your opponent's hotels. You'd like to buy houses, but with a bad roll you'd have to tear them down. Beyond Boardwalk doesn't let you hedge your bet. If you want to buy houses, buy them now or wait until your next turn. This is like modern real estate deals—timing is everything.

Tax Time

Rule 11. *If you land on Income Tax, you can count your money before deciding whether to pay $200 or 10 percent.*

Sorry, we haven't repealed the Income Tax. You still have to pay either $200 or 10 percent of your net worth. But we have repealed the rule that makes you pick your option before counting your money. Donald Trump hires a team of accountants to keep track of his money. Why should you have to guess?

Part Two

Playing to Win

Chapter 3

Basic Strategy

"I am a man of principle, and my first principle is flexibility."

—Senator Everett Dirksen

Okay. You like the new rules. You've dusted off your board and invited your neighbors over for a friendly game. All you need to know is: How can you put those "friends" into the poorhouse? Time for some basic strategy.

How Much Money Do You Have?

The answer is: less than you think. In Monopoly®, the early part of the game is a breeze. You cruise carefree around the board, buying everything, with minimal risk. It's not uncommon to find, after a few times around the board, that each player has six or seven properties plus a reasonable amount of cash.

Beyond Boardwalk is a lot more exciting, and a lot more dangerous. Because of the auction, properties tend to cost far more than list price early on. So you'd better be selective or you can die young. In one game, our friend Dave got off to a flying start against two more seasoned opponents. During his first trip around the board he had bought two orange properties, as well as the only two railroads that had been landed on. His game plan was clear: Use the railroads to generate cash. Try to buy a third or fourth railroad. And do whatever he could to acquire that orange monopoly.

In Monopoly®, Dave's properties would have cost only $780 ($400 for the two railroads, $200 for New York Avenue, and $180 for St. James). Since each player starts with $1,500, Dave would have had $720 left as he approached Go for the first time. But in Beyond Boardwalk, competitive bidding drives prices up. As a result, Dave had spent $1,300 for his four properties, leaving him with just $200.

When Dave landed on Pennsylvania Avenue—list price $320, minimum bid $170—he cautiously bid $180, confident he wouldn't get stuck with it at that price. Two hundred dollars said one opponent, and the other raised the ante to $225. Encouraged by their show of interest, Dave bid $230, just to keep the bidding going. Then—dead silence. Both opponents passed, and Dave was stuck. To buy Pennsylvania, a property he didn't want, he was forced to sell one of his railroads. His cash position got even worse on the next turn, when he landed on the merciless Luxury Tax—$75. Just ten minutes into the game Dave was nearly broke, and he never recovered.

The moral is simple: You can't afford to make a bad purchase. Most properties sell for more than list price, and you may soon find yourself short of cash. So how much money do you have? Usually just barely enough to buy what you desperately need—a single monopoly, and maybe a few railroads if you're lucky.

Why Some Squares Are More Equal Than Others

If money is so tight, you'd better buy smart. What makes for a good property? Two things: the probability of landing, and the return on investment. You may have noticed in playing Monopoly® that nobody ever seemed to land on your prized Boardwalk/Park Place monopoly, while modest properties in the middle of the board attracted much more traffic. That was not just sour grapes. The most important result of the computer revolution is that the probability of landing on each square can be determined. Professor Irvin Hentzel of Iowa State University has done precisely that, and has graciously allowed us to reprint a table that summarizes his findings. The table ranks all forty squares, from the most to the least landed-on:

PROPERTY	PROBABILITY OF LANDING
1. Jail/Just Visiting	.0698*
2. Illinois Avenue	.0355
3. Go	.0346
4. B & O Railroad	.0343
5. Free Parking	.0335
6. Tennessee Avenue	.0335
7. New York Avenue	.0334
8. Reading Railroad	.0332
9. St. James Place	.0318
10. Water Works	.0315
11. Pennsylvania Railroad	.0313
12. Kentucky Avenue	.0310
13. Electric Company	.0310
14. Indiana Avenue	.0305
15. St. Charles Place	.0303
16. Atlantic Avenue	.0301
17. Pacific Avenue	.0300
18. Ventnor Avenue	.0299
19. Boardwalk	.0295
20. North Carolina Avenue	.0293
21. Marvin Gardens	.0289
22. Virginia Avenue	.0288
23. Pennsylvania Avenue	.0279
24. Community Chest (square 17)	.0272
25. Short Line Railroad	.0272
26. Community Chest (square 33)	.0264
27. Income Tax	.0260

*We have assumed that players will always get out of Jail immediately. Since a player occasionally stays in Jail for one or two turns, the true probability for the Jail/Just Visiting square is actually a little higher.

28. Vermont Avenue	.0260
29. States Avenue	.0258
30. Connecticut Avenue	.0257
31. Oriental Avenue	.0253
32. Park Place	.0244
33. Luxury Tax	.0244
34. Baltic Avenue	.0242
35. Mediterranean Avenue	.0238
36. Community Chest (square 2)	.0211
37. Chance (square 22)	.0124†
38. Chance (square 36)	.0097
39. Chance (square 7)	.0097
40. Go To Jail	.0000‡

The probability chart is full of juicy information:

The Crowded Jails

The most striking finding is that Jail/Just Visiting is by far the most popular spot on the board. Like it or not, you're going to spend a lot of time either behind bars or "just visiting" your convict friends. There are five ways to wind up on this single square:

1. By landing on Just Visiting with the regular roll of the dice.
2. By landing on the Go To Jail square.
3. By rolling doubles three times in a row.
4. By drawing the "Go To Jail" *Chance* card.
5. By drawing the "Go To Jail" *Community Chest* card.

---

†The probabilities for Chance are so low because ten of the sixteen *Chance* cards direct you to move your token to another square. By contrast, only two of the sixteen *Community Chest* cards direct you to move your token, and only two of the twelve *Go* cards. This table does not reflect the minor effect that that those *Go* cards have on landing probabilities.

‡Since the Go To Jail square sends you immediately to Jail, it's impossible to stay there, so the probability is listed as zero.

Stuck in the Middle Again

If you look at the fifteen names that follow Jail on the probability chart, you will notice a striking pattern: Thirteen of the fifteen lie on the middle two sides of the board. There may be forty squares in Monopoly®, but most of the action is in the eighteen between Jail and Water Works. Just as in basketball or chess, the player who controls the middle controls the game.

The main reason for this pattern is the traffic pouring out of Jail. Because Jail is landed on so frequently, the properties that lie a roll or two beyond that square—such as Illinois Avenue and B & O—attract a lot of visitors. In addition, the Go To Jail square acts as a barrier, keeping players corralled in the middle two sides of the board.

Because of all the traffic, the orange and red monopolies are especially valuable. The three orange properties—Tennessee, New York, and St. James—rank sixth, seventh, and ninth among the forty squares on the board. The reds—Illinois, Kentucky, and Indiana—rank second, twelfth, and fourteenth. After players have seen the probability chart, they will gladly pay more than list price for the orange and red properties.

All Aboard!

The other standout properties are the railroads. Of the thirteen squares landed on most frequently, five are "railroads".* Rail service may be declining in the United States, but in the world of Beyond Boardwalk, everyone takes the train. If you can acquire four or five railroads, you are almost certain to strike it rich.

---

*Short Line is the ugly duckling among the six railroads. It lies on the fourth row of the board, outside the heavily traveled corridor between Jail and Water Works. In addition, Short Line does not benefit from the *Chance* cards saying "Advance token to the nearest Railroad," since there is no Chance square between B & O and Short Line. As a result, Short Line ranks a lowly twenty-fifth on the probability chart.

It's All in the Cards

The *Chance* and *Community Chest* cards have a significant effect on landing probabilities. Four properties are honored with their own *Chance* cards: Illinois Avenue, Reading Railroad, St. Charles Place, and Boardwalk. There are also two cards saying "Advance token to the nearest Railroad" and one saying "Advance token to nearest utility." These cards direct traffic to Reading Railroad, Electric Company, Pennsylvania Railroad, B & O Railroad, and Water Works.

All eight properties affected by the *Chance* cards appear among the top twenty squares on the board. Meanwhile, the Chance squares themselves are at the bottom of the list, since ten of the sixteen *Chance* cards direct you to move your token elsewhere.

The Plight of the Slumlord

Mediterranean and Baltic, besides paying the lowest rents, are also landed on less often than any other properties. So Mediterranean is even less valuable than you thought. The other low-rent properties—Oriental, Vermont, and Connecticut—also appear at the tail end of the chart.

It's Lonely at the Top

Boardwalk and Park Place are the most glamorous properties—but they may also be the most overrated. Boardwalk, with the aid of a *Chance* card, ranks nineteenth. Park Place is buried in thirty-second place, barely ahead of Baltic and Mediterranean. So if you felt lonely in your penthouse suite, it wasn't just your imagination. Park Place has a list price of $350, but in games involving knowledgeable players, it is often sold for $250 or less.

The Art of Investment

Before you bid $1,000 for Illinois Avenue, remember: Landing probabilities are only part of the story. Even if players landed on Mediterranean Avenue on every turn, you wouldn't get far by collecting the paltry $5 in rent. The other part of the story is: What is the return on investment?

Let's take a couple of extreme examples: Connecticut Avenue and Pennsylvania Avenue. Connecticut Avenue is a slum. The sidewalks are cracking, the porches need repair, and you find broken bottles on your doorstep every Sunday morning. The list price is $120, rent is $10, and you can build houses for just $50 each. Pennsylvania Avenue is a ritzy place, with five-acre lots, three-car garages, and a swimming pool behind every house. You pay for these privileges. List price is $320, rent is $30, and building just one luxurious house will cost you $200. Snob appeal aside, is Pennsylvania Avenue a good investment?

Let's take a look at the rate of return for housing on both properties:

	CONNECTICUT AVENUE	PENNSYLVANIA AVENUE
Cost per house	$ 50	$ 200
Rent with 1 house	40	150
with 2 houses	100	450
with 3 houses	300	1,000
with 4 houses	450	1,200
with hotel	600	1,400

The results say a lot about the strategy of Beyond Boardwalk:

• *Cheap properties can pay off*. The great advantage of the light-blues is that you can build houses cheaply—only $50 each. If the light-blues are available at list price, $320 will buy you the entire monopoly. For another $200, you can build four houses on Connecticut Avenue. The rent with four houses is $450—a nice return on your investment. To earn $450 with the greens, you have to spend $1,320. That's a big difference.

• *It pays to build three houses.* In both groups, your best investment is buying the third house. With Connecticut, that $50 house triples the rent, from $100 to $300. With Pennsylvania, you spend $200 for the third house, but the rent soars from $450 to $1,000. This pattern is repeated everywhere around the board—three houses are always a lot better than two.

So, it is crucial to consider the rate of return before buying property. If there's an auction for Pennsylvania Avenue, don't get starry-eyed about the potential of earning $1,400 if you build a hotel. Ask yourself: Do I have any realistic chance of coming up with the thousands of dollars it may take to develop the greens fully? If the answer is yes, bid away. But if you're one step away from the poorhouse, Pennsylvania Avenue is no bargain.

Chapter 4

Early Game

"The great mistake made by the public is paying attention to prices instead of values."

—C. H. Dow

In Monopoly®, there is little strategy, especially early in the game. The goal is simple: Buy everything. In Beyond Boardwalk you have to start thinking with the first roll of the dice. You can't afford to buy everything, so you'd better be selective. The key to the early game is: Keep your eyes open, assess your opponents' strategies, and buy smart.

To Buy or Not to Buy?

The board is set up, the phone answering machine is on, and the refrigerator is full. It's time for your first roll. You throw a six—Oriental Avenue. List price: $100. You can buy it outright for $200, you can open the bidding (minimum bid $60), or you can pass. What should you do?

You may be thinking: *I'll buy it for $200*. And why not? You'd like to own some property and this will give you a jump on the other players. You have $1,500 in cash, and it's already burning a hole in your pocket. Sure, Oriental is a bit of a slum, but it has—well, it has potential. Just clear out the debris in front, spruce up the neighborhood with a few trees, and pretty soon you'll be ready to build a shiny new development.

Well, you're right. Oriental does have potential. The exciting part about the early game is that *every* property has potential. Any property can turn out to be the foundation of your future empire. But since you can't buy everything, it may help to consider the ways in which a property can help you win:

1. Monopoly value: A property is most valuable when it gives you a monopoly. But you don't obtain a monopoly all at once. Buying Oriental could be the first step.
2. Defensive value: If you own a property, the square becomes safe for you. You will never have to pay rent and nobody else will be able to build houses on it. The defensive value is highest if another player needs the property to complete a monopoly. But even early in the game, once you buy Oriental, nobody else can obtain the monopoly unless he deals with you.
3. Rental value: Every property pays some rent, even if you don't own a monopoly. You can poke fun at the $10 that Oriental brings you, but sometimes it can save you from disaster.
4. Trade value: Any property can be traded for another property that is worth more to you.
5. Resale value: Any property can be sold to another player. In addition, you can sell property to the Bank for one-half the list price. Resale value is especially promising if a property is available cheap. Suppose, for example, you can buy Pacific Avenue (list price $300) for the minimum bid of $160. You can resell Pacific to the Bank at any time for $150—just $10 less than you paid for it. If you manage to collect rent just once, at $30, you have made a profit of $20. If you're forced to sell it back (for $150) before collecting rent, you have still lost only $10.

Early in the game, before you have a monopoly to develop, buying property is your best investment. There are no money-market funds in Beyond Boardwalk. The only sure way to make money is in real estate.

So what should you do about Oriental Avenue? If it gives you a monopoly, buy it outright for $200. But early in the game, you should allow it to be auctioned off. You'll find that the top bid is usually $150 or less.

The Joy of Bidding

Bidding is lots of fun. You're competing directly against the other players, conducting a running argument about what each property is worth. And very often, at the end of the auction, every player feels that he has won. The high bidder thinks Atlantic Avenue is a steal for $400. The other players are chuckling to themselves about their skill at bluffing. They know they wouldn't have wanted it even for the list price of $260.

One key to successful bidding is to know your opponents. The first few auctions will tell you a lot about them. Sometimes a novice goes on a wild buying spree, determined to buy every property. Be patient. Bait him a little to push the prices up, but don't try to outbid him. He will soon be short of money and will be a minor factor in future auctions.

Auctions are trickier when other players share your sense of property values. One crucial tactic is to force an opponent to pay top dollar for a property that you didn't want in the first place. Watch him carefully: Is he raising your bid eagerly, $50 at a time, or is he reluctantly raising the ante $5 at a time? You might want him to pay $400 for St. James Place, but how would you feel getting stuck for $395? It's rewarding to deplete your opponent's cash, but when you play with fire, you're bound to get burned sometimes.

Intelligent bidding wins games. Every property has value to someone; it is your task to assess what the value is and how you might benefit. The rule of thumb is to make sure you get

Going . . . Going . . . Gone!

the properties you need—or, failing that, to force an opponent to ruin *his* cash position in an all-out effort to stop you.

After a few games, even the most aggressive player will recognize that he can't control the game by himself. You can't buy everything you need and still prevent every other player from getting a monopoly. Defensive play is important, but you can only play defense sparingly. If you spend all your money on blocking everyone else, you won't have any left to develop your own monopoly.

That brings us to the ultimate art of Beyond Boardwalk: the art of *talking*. Whether you are bidding, trading, or simply trying to con someone into doing something he thinks is dangerous, you've got to know how to communicate. The psychological skills of a Beyond Boardwalk player are every bit as important as the rolls of the dice. Consider, for instance, defensive bidding—stopping an opponent from completing a monopoly. You know it has to be done, but wouldn't you be happier if it were done with someone else's money? A well-placed suggestion might persuade an opponent to shoulder the burden.

Therefore, in this aspect of the game—as in all others—never underestimate the power of the spoken word. But remember, it works both ways. Most salesmen say their favorite customer is another salesman.

Hiding Your Cash

Maybe you're open by nature. You tell your friends everything. You tell your boss you were out playing golf when everyone else in your foursome called in sick. You throw open-house parties. You even have an open marriage.

Well, it's time for you to hide something. You must not let your opponents see how much money you have. If you've just bid $250 for a railroad, and the whole world knows you've got

$25 in cash, you are in big trouble. Bluffing is a big part of Beyond Boardwalk, but you can't fool anyone if your money is stacked neatly into piles in front of you.

Meanwhile, you must keep tabs on your opponents' cash flow. Not literally, of course—this isn't the CIA. But you should exploit every legitimate opportunity to assess your opponents' wealth:

1. Early in the game: Everyone starts with the same amount of money—$1,500. For at least the first time around the board, you should have a good sense of how much money the other players have left. Often, at least one player will have next to nothing by the time he reaches Go.

2. Tax time: When you land on Income Tax, you have to pay either $200 or 10 percent of your net worth. If an opponent pays less than $200, you will be able to calculate his or her cash position exactly. If he pays $200, you will know what he has at a minimum.

3. Telltale signs of poverty: The resale of either houses or property to the Bank is the surest sign of poverty. If a player needs to sell a house to pay you $5 rent for Mediterranean, you know where he stands. A sudden change in a player's bidding strategy is also a good sign that his bankroll is not what it used to be.

The Railroads: Early Muscle

Early in the game, the most intriguing properties are the six railroads. With just three railroads, you earn $100 every time someone lands. With four, you are up to $200. Assuming that nobody gets a quick monopoly, a player with three railroads often becomes the richest player in the game; a player with four almost always does.

Rail Baron at Work

How much are the railroads worth? In the early game, railroads sell for \$350-\$400—a significant premium over their \$200 Monopoly® price. Do they pay off? It depends on how many you acquire. If you can buy four railroads, you are in a very strong position. Having four properties that generate \$200 each is practically a guarantee against being knocked out early. It may not win the game by itself, but you will have a leg up in acquiring a monopoly or fighting for the fifth and sixth railroads. The other advantage of owning four or more railroads is that you always pose a threat. The other players are in danger of hitting you all around the board.

There is one catch: It is very difficult to obtain that fourth railroad. Once you own even two, the other players will do almost anything to stop you from buying more. And one of the worst positions in Beyond Boardwalk is to be stopped in your tracks with three railroads. You've invested as much as \$1,200—four fifths of your initial stake—in just three properties, without owning even a share of a monopoly. The \$100 rental income pales in comparison with what other players can charge as they obtain and develop monopolies. So if you want to be a rail baron, don't stop at three. Do whatever you can to obtain a fourth railroad, and a fifth and sixth if possible. If you seem stuck at three, try dealing with another player to get the cash or properties you need to obtain a monopoly.

The Scrooge Strategy

Lack of money is the root of all evil, says the capitalist. So why not skip the early bidding altogether and hold on to your beloved bankroll? Then you can swoop in after your reckless friends impoverish one another.

With the help of a grant from the Beyond Boardwalk Foundation, we have researched this strategy thoroughly. And we're glad to report it doesn't work—at least not in its most radical form. The Scrooge Strategy has three problems:

1. Sitting out the auctions doesn't mean that you conserve all your wealth. As others acquire property—especially railroads—your cash may be depleted by those nasty rent bills.
2. You are taking the risk that another player will establish a dominant position before you even begin to bid. As a dyed-in-the-wool hoarder, you are foregoing your *defensive* responsibilities as well. The other players may not be able to block an aggressive bidder by themselves.
3. Even if nobody else becomes dominant, you may find that the bargains you were counting on just don't exist. Sure, the other players may let you buy Vermont Avenue—as long as one player already owns Connecticut and another one owns Oriental. But those leftovers won't help you much. As soon as you threaten to acquire a monopoly, the bidding will suddenly heat up again. When it comes to the properties you really need, you'll have to pay the premium prices you thought you could avoid by sitting out the early bidding.

Surviving in a Crowded World

Have you ever looked for an apartment in New York or San Francisco? A studio costs $700 or more—if you can find one. The reason is simple: supply and demand. Every day, hordes of apartment hunters hit the streets at dawn, searching for the rare bargain.

In Beyond Boardwalk, four-player games are spirited and competitive. But with five or six players it's the law of the jun-

gle. There's more demand but the same fixed supply of properties; as a result, prices soar. Since you can afford to buy only
four or five properties, you can't afford to make mistakes. You
need to take even more extreme measures to acquire an early
monopoly because you may not get a second chance.

In six-player games the radical strategies work best. A
player who very aggressively buys and develops the first monopoly can quickly eliminate opponents who were equally
reckless but less successful. Meanwhile, the extremely conser-
vative player may still be around to buy property at bargain
prices after the first couple of players go broke.

Chapter 5

Middle Game

"A fool and his money are soon parted. What I want
to know is how they got together in the first place."
—Cyril Fletcher

The key to the middle game is obtaining and developing the
right monopoly. Be single-minded. There is no prize for accu-
mulating a rainbow of title deeds from different color groups.
You must buy, sell, trade, cajole, beg—do whatever it takes to
get that monopoly.

Stating the principle is one thing; applying it is another.
Here are some tips:

• *Don't be too defensive.* You should try to stop other
players from completing a monopoly. But realistically that
means forcing them to pay a premium price for the last property, or making sure they have to deal with you to get it. In most
games every player eventually obtains at least one monopoly.
Even Dwight Gooden would have trouble throwing a shutout in
Beyond Boardwalk. The goal is not to keep your opponents at
zero but to outscore them by having the best and most highly
developed monopoly.

• *Don't get distracted.* Suppose you have Indiana, Kentucky, and two yellows. Someone lands on Illinois and decides
to go to auction; this is your chance for a monopoly. Then you
count your cash—$80. How can you even enter the bidding?
The answer is simple: by selling or trading your two yellows.

You can either deal with another player or return them to the Bank for $130 each. Sure, you may have spent $300 for each one. Sure, it would be nice to have both the reds *and* the yellows. But the challenge of Beyond Boardwalk is making choices. You need a monopoly, and this isn't poker: You can't win with two pairs—unless one of the pairs is Boardwalk and Park Place.

In Search of the Perfect Monopoly

Beyond Boardwalk encourages greed: more money, more power, more land. Temptation always beckons. Sooner or later you may be faced with the prospect of owning two monopolies instead of just one. Maybe you *can* have it all.

If you can, more power to you. But Beyond Boardwalk is a lot like real life—usually you are forced to choose. Which monopoly do you want?

The answer depends partly on the structure of the game at that moment, partly on the trades that may be available. But here are a few rules of thumb:

• *Remember the landing probabilities*. The properties flanking Free Parking—the oranges and the reds—attract the most traffic. There's no point in building houses if nobody stops to pay rent.

• *Cheap properties can pay off*. In the middle game most players are short on cash. At $200 per house, building on Pennsylvania or Boardwalk may be a pipe dream. Even if you can build a little, you may not be able to reach the three-house level, where an investment begins to earn a good return. So most of the time you are better off avoiding the luxury properties if you have the opportunity to build elsewhere.

There's another good reason for preferring the low-rent

district: Suppose you have to sell houses back to the Bank. The Bank drives a hard bargain. It pays you only half the cost of the house. If you bought a house for $50, you receive only $25 when you sell it back. If you paid $200 for the house, you turn in it for $100.

How does this affect your choice of monopolies? The sad fact about Beyond Boardwalk is that you are usually strapped for cash. You may need to sell a house just to pay a $10 rent bill. And if that happens, you're better off selling a $50 house for $25 than a $200 house for $100.

• *On every side of the board, aim for the monopoly that is farther from Go.* Houses on the orange properties cost $100, just like houses on the maroons. But the oranges always pay more, as shown by this chart:

RENT	ST. CHARLES PLACE	ST. JAMES PLACE
With one house	$ 50	$ 70
With two houses	150	200
With three houses	450	550
With four houses	625	750
With hotel	750	950

This pattern is repeated on every side of the board: within each row, the properties that are farther from Go pay more rent. With or without houses, Connecticut is better than Baltic, St. James is more chic than St. Charles, and Boardwalk is more profitable than Pennsylvania.

• *Choose a monopoly that can win the game for you.* The monopolies between St. Charles Place and Pennsylvania are landed on frequently, and they pay a minimum of $750 with a hotel. Once you develop these properties, they can deliver a knockout blow with a single roll of the dice.

What about the other three monopolies—the dark-purples (Mediterranean and Baltic), the light-blues, and the dark-blues? They all have problems. The worst properties, by far, are Mediterranean and Baltic. They are landed on infrequently. They pay the lowest rent—just $250 for a hotel on Mediterranean, $450 for Baltic. They are located immediately after Go, which means that your opponent will have at least $200 in hand when he lands on you. And the rate of return is terrible, especially for Mediterranean:

RATE OF RETURN ON MEDITERRANEAN AVENUE

	HOUSING INVESTMENT	RENT	RATE OF RETURN
One house	$ 50	$ 10	20%
Two houses	100	30	30%
Three houses	150	90	60%
Four houses	200	160	80%
Hotel	250	250	100%

Compare these rates to the rates for other properties: houses on New York Avenue, for example, earn from 80 percent to 200 percent on investment. At each level of building, Mediterranean offers the worst return of any property on the board.

The light-blues also suffer from low landing probability, bad location, and low rent: just $550 for a hotel on Oriental and Vermont, $600 for Connecticut. It's tough to knock someone out when your biggest punch delivers only $600 worth of damage, and when you can't land it very often. If the light-blues are your only monopoly, by all means build, but you will have trouble winning with the light-blues alone.

The vaunted dark-blues—Boardwalk and Park Place—are also flawed. The obvious problem is the high cost of development—$200 per house. But even with the cash, you may have problems. Boardwalk and Park Place are not visited very often. And there are only two properties in the monopoly.

The dark-blues, though, have one saving grace. The rate of return is wonderful—especially on Boardwalk:

RATE OF RETURN ON BOARDWALK

	HOUSING INVESTMENT	RENT	RATE OF RETURN
One house	$ 200	$ 200	100%
Two houses	400	600	150%
Three houses	600	1,400	233%
Four houses	800	1,700	212%
Hotel	1,000	2,000	200%

The 233 percent return with three houses represents the best rate of return on the whole board. The problem is: If nobody lands on you, you will never collect, and you won't win.

The Psychology of Trading

Making deals is a big part of Beyond Boardwalk. Occasionally you will be able to buy everything you need at the auctions and ignore all offers to trade. Most of the time, though, you won't win if you don't trade. Shrewd trading can overcome early mistakes or misfortune at the auction block.

Skillful trading requires a keen sense of property values. But you'll also need to master the psychology of trading. By knowing whom to deal with, and when to deal, you can often turn trades to your advantage. Here are a few tips:

• *Know your opponents.* Everyone plays Monopoly® a little differently. Some players love to take risks, while others try to amass a big cash reserve. Some players like the railroads, while others enjoy the cachet of Boardwalk. Even the most rational players usually have an emotional attachment to one set of properties or one style of play. If you know the quirks of your opponents, you have a strong psychological advantage when it comes time to trade.

• *The weakest player is your best friend.* As President Reagan has often pointed out, you need to bargain from a posi-

tion of strength. In Beyond Boardwalk, that means finding
someone who's weaker than you are. If you're in fifth place,
start chatting with the poor sucker in sixth. If you're down to
your last $50, find the player who is down to his last $5. He
might not like what you're proposing, but what choice does he
have? If he doesn't make a deal, he's sure to lose. The trade
you're suggesting might shake up the game enough to give him
a chance.

• *Pick your spots*. There comes a time when even a
stronger player may feel desperate. Suppose, for example, that
another player owns the yellow monopoly and Connecticut
Avenue. You have Oriental and Vermont. You've offered to
buy Connecticut for $250, but he's laughed you off. Why
should he let you have a monopoly? Bide your time. At some
point, he may be faced with a sudden need for cash—to pay
rent, to buy property, or to build houses. Offer him a rock-
bottom price. At that point, he may have no choice but to accept.

• *Use extortion*. Suppose you have a monopoly, plus two
railroads. You also have a small problem: You're flat broke.
Meanwhile, Robin the Rail Baron has four railroads, and Mary
the Monopolist is building on the yellows. You desperately
need cash to keep up with them.

Your best move is to sell the railroads to Mary, since Robin,
with six railroads, could charge $400 per ride. But when you
talk to Mary, her eyes glaze over. She couldn't care less about
your railroads; she wants to win with her yellows. There may be
a way to pique her interest: Threaten to sell the railroads to
Robin. Force Mary to pay you $500 for the privilege of collect-
ing $50 in rent. You'll get the cash you need, and your world
will actually become safer, since she will have less money to
invest in houses.

This strategy is particularly effective if Mary is a defensive
player who is deathly afraid of seeing Robin get the six rail-

roads. Your risk, of course, is that Mary may spurn your offer, or else accept the offer and then sell the railroads to Robin. But extortion can be so effective that you should rarely close a deal with the obvious trading partner until you sound out the other players.

- *"We're all in this together."* Sometimes you are in a bind. The weakest player refuses to deal with you. Or even worse, *you're* the weakest player, and your opponents are trying to bleed you dry. This is the time to try camaraderie. Remind your friends of all the good times you've shared together. Act as if you're one big family, working together to defeat that ogre who happens to be winning at the moment. Your opponents may be skeptical about this sudden show of goodwill. Keep trying. Your only alternative is to face extinction alone. As Samuel Johnson said, the prospect of hanging can focus the mind wonderfully.

- *Cut your losses.* Sometimes you'll need to trade to compensate for an early mistake. Suppose you bid $500 for Illinois to prevent someone else from getting a monopoly. You've been broke ever since, and now you're on the verge of bankruptcy. Meanwhile, your opponent has gone on to bigger and better monopolies. We've seen players in this situation refuse to make a reasonable trade. "I paid $500 for this property," they say, "and I won't sell it for less." This statement is like banging your shoe on the table. It's fine as a bargaining ploy, but don't let your earlier mistake force you into another one. If bluster doesn't work, calm down and accept the best deal you can find. It may be the only way to stay in the game.

The Cash Advantage

Most trades center on the exchange of property. There may be extended negotiations, but eventually you approach an agreement—you'll trade two reds for her yellow. At this point your opponent will start to look eager. She's already imagining how good Illinois would look with a few houses. After all the bargaining, she is psychologically committed to making the trade. This is the time to ask for something extra: cash on the barrelhead. It doesn't have to be a lot—$150 or $200 will do. If you're too greedy, she'll balk at the whole idea of throwing in money.

Even $150 can make a big difference. That money represents one more house for you, and one less for her. If someone lands on your property with the house there, your cash advantage is immediately multiplied.

Besides, there is nothing more frustrating than owning a monopoly without having the cash to develop it. In Beyond Boardwalk, where money is always a problem, this plight is common. By seeking the cash advantage in every trade, you can avoid the cash squeeze. Let your opponent feel the sting of being land-rich but cash-poor.

Creative Trading

There used to be only two flavors of ice cream: chocolate and vanilla. And there used to be only two things to offer in a trade: money or property. Times have changed. Kids grow up with boysenberry ice cream and Swiss almond crunch. And Beyond Boardwalk offers its own variations on the plain old vanilla trade. Here are some suggestions for adding flavor to your big deals:

• *Free rides:* This gives you immunity if you land on someone else's property. Suppose you're trading two railroads to a player who already owns four. With six, he will be able to charge $400 every time someone gets on board. That could be good news—the rail baron will put pressure on other players.

The problem, of course, is that you will inevitably land on one of the railroads. The solution: Negotiate for one or more "free rides," so that you can land on the railroads and pay no rent.

• *The invisible hand:* You can retain some control over a property even after you've traded it to another player. Suppose that Matt owns three railroads, you own one, and Barbara owns none. You need cash, but you don't want to put a fourth railroad in Matt's hands. You would like to sell it to Barbara, but you're afraid that she will turn around and sell it to Matt. One solution is to sell the railroad to Barbara, but only if she agrees that she will never sell it to Matt.

Your "invisible hand" can also control another player's right to build. If you make a trade that gives a monopoly to another player, you can make him agree not to build houses for a certain number of turns, or until you acquire a monopoly.

• *Right of first refusal:* This gives you the right to match any competing cash offer if another player decides to sell a particular property. For example, if you own Pacific and North Carolina, and Corinne owns Pennsylvania Avenue, you can obtain from Corinne a right of first refusal on Pennsylvania. She can keep Pennsylvania for as long as she wants, but if she ever decides to sell it, you have the right to buy it by matching the highest offer.

• *Insurance:* You can buy "insurance" from another player against an unfavorable roll of the dice. Suppose that your token is on Baltic Avenue. Your opponent owns a hotel on Connecticut, just six squares away. If you land there, the rent is $600. To minimize your risk, you can offer the other player a "premium"—maybe $100—to give you immunity from having to pay rent if you roll a six. It can be a good deal for both players— you get peace of mind, and he pockets $100.

How much is insurance worth? That depends on two factors:

1. The amount of rent you would have to pay if you landed on the property.
2. The probability of landing on the property.

Here are the odds of rolling each number, from two to twelve:

Two: 1 in 36 (2.8%)
Three: 2 in 36 (5.6%)
Four: 3 in 36 (8.3%)
Five: 4 in 36 (11.1%)
Six: 5 in 36 (13.9%)
Seven: 6 in 36 (16.7%)
Eight: 5 in 36 (13.9%)
Nine: 4 in 36 (11.1%)
Ten: 3 in 36 (8.3%)
Eleven: 2 in 36 (5.6%)
Twelve: 1 in 36 (2.8%)

The greater the chance of landing on another player's property, the more you should be willing to pay for insurance. The odds can be pretty high on some rolls. Suppose you are five, seven, and eight squares away from three hotels. Your odds of hitting one of them are 15 in 36, or 41.7 percent.

• *Partnerships:* Partnerships let you share the income from a property with another player. Suppose you have cash but no monopoly. You own Boardwalk and have your eye on Park Place. Your opponent has no use for Park Place; his only reason to keep it is to block you. In exchange for Park Place, offer him a permanent free ride on both Boardwalk and Park Place. And here's the sweetener: He gets some of the rent you collect on both properties. You pay the cost of building houses—all he does is share in the profits. Even if you give him a one-third share, your houses can make him rich. If someone lands on Boardwalk with three houses, you and he will be dividing a rent payment of $1,400.

A word of caution: Giving away permanent free rides can be dangerous. If you and your partner are the last two players in the game, and he has a free ride on all of your property, you are almost sure to lose. Also, while partnerships are legal, they aren't much fun. They slow down the game and undermine its capitalist spirit.

• *Pay another player not to bid.* * Suppose there's an auction for Pacific Avenue, a property you desperately need. Marc seems too poor to bid, but Andy might give you trouble. Ask Andy to give up his right to bid in exchange for either cash or property. But beware—the trade makes sense only if your perceptions are accurate. If Andy is not as rich as you think, you may be giving him something for nothing. And if Marc is not as poor, the auction could still wind up costing you a bundle.

You can also ask someone not to bid in a *future* auction. If you are making a trade to acquire Park Place, you can ask your opponent to relinquish his right to bid on Boardwalk if it becomes available. This kind of "futures" contract can be made even if Boardwalk is already owned, since the property might be sold back to the Bank and then become available later in the game.

Build You Must

Building houses is the surest way to win in Beyond Boardwalk. If you earn $500 or more in rent, you deliver a crushing blow to your opponent and acquire the means to hit him even harder the next time. But building is always a risk. The board is a dangerous place in the middle game; the other players have

---

*This option is available only if you decide to permit trades that affect players' rights in the auction. This variation slows down the game slightly but adds some spice to the auction itself.

either developed their monopolies or accumulated enough rail-roads to give you motion sickness on every ride. If you land on someone else's property, you may need to sell houses just to pay the rent. And selling houses for half their original price is painful.

So what can you do? You have to take a chance and build anyway. That doesn't mean buying houses when you're approaching a row of your opponents' hotels or when their tokens are nowhere near your property. There's no point in throwing money away. But it does mean that you have to accept some risk, develop your property . . . and pray before you roll the dice.

One Monopoly at a Time

Some players assume that if one monopoly is good, two must be better. They spend money pursuing a second monopoly instead of developing the first. But hard experience proves them wrong. There is no time in the middle game for acquiring excess property. Once you have a monopoly, the best place to invest your money is in houses—at least until you have three houses on each property. You are better off making your mark with one monopoly than you are spreading a few houses all over the board.

Chapter 6

End Game

"I don't meet the competition. I destroy it."
—Charles Revson

In the end game, winning is everything. You're not looking for a slight edge or trying to consolidate a long-term position. Now is the time to bankrupt your opponents. At this point the board is filled with land mines—properties with rents high enough to deliver a mortal blow. It's still okay to make trades or to team up temporarily with another player, but remember: Your goal is to put everyone else out of the game.

Your Money or Your Deeds—How to Collect

If you own property that commands exorbitant rent, your opponent may be in trouble when he lands on you. Generally, his cash on hand will not be enough to pay the bill—he will have poured most of his money into buying houses. His only choices are: Sell houses back to the Bank, sell property to the Bank or to another player, or try to trade with you.

So he looks at you slyly and tries to sound nonchalant. He wants to know: How about making a deal?

Should you accept property or free rides instead of cash? The answer, almost always, is no. If you insist on cash, your opponent may never recover. He may never again be able to develop his property to its former grandeur. He may, in fact, be on his way out of the game.

But there are times when not being paid can pay off:

1. If your monopoly is fully developed and your opponent can give you a second monopoly. Suppose you've built hotels on the reds and you have plenty of cash. Your only other property is Atlantic Avenue. You've been trying for half an hour to pry the other two yellows from your opponent. Now that he's resting uneasily in an Illinois motel, he may be willing to talk.

2. If your opponent has railroads. The beauty of the railroads is that they generate cash instantly, without your having to spend money building houses. If your opponent owns two or more railroads, consider accepting them as part of a deal.

3. If your most powerful opponent is just sitting back, watching the fun. Suppose Edward, owner of the maroons (with a few houses), two railroads, and $300 in cash, has just checked in at the New York Hilton. Clearly, Edward is on his last legs. Ron, who has hotels on the reds, poses the real threat. Instead of pushing Edward to the brink of bankruptcy, why not use him as a tool to beat Ron? Consider accepting the railroads plus a liberal supply of free rides on the maroons, with the goal of keeping Edward in the game. If you're lucky, Ron will visit Edward's maroons several times before Edward is finally eliminated. Meanwhile, Edward poses no threat to you: you have the free rides!

Doing Time

In Beyond Boardwalk, it's usually smart to get out of Jail in a hurry. When you're behind bars you can't bid on property

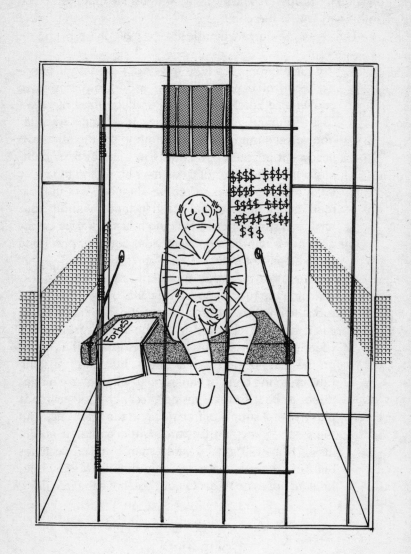

Doing Time

and you collect only half the usual rent. But at the end of the game, you may need to use your Jail time strategically.

Suppose, for example, that you have developed the green monopoly, and your opponents have developed the orange and red. In addition, they have just passed Go—they're nowhere near your property.

Why rush to get out of Jail? Your first taste of freedom could lead you straight to the St. James Hotel. Give your opponents time to approach your property. Give them a chance to land on each other, which might cause some of those menacing houses to come tumbling down. Why not find a good book in the prison library and serve out your full term in peace?

Bargain Hunting

Late in the game, the "bargains" appear. Most players will have sold their surplus properties back to the Bank to raise money for houses. When someone lands on one of these properties, it will be available—cheap. You will often be able to buy property for just half the list price plus $10—the minimum bid. It's easy to be tempted. New York for $110? Park Place for $185? Who can resist?

If you're smart, you can. That $110 investment in New York may look cheap. It may earn you some money, since if someone lands even once, you are guaranteed a profit (rent is $20, and you can always sell the property back to the Bank for $100). All the same, buying New York Avenue is probably not the best way to invest your money. If you already own the maroon monopoly, that $110 could be used to buy a house on States Avenue, which will earn far more than $20 the next time someone visits.

It's not that New York Avenue is a *bad* investment. It's simply a matter of timing. If you must choose between housing and land, find yourself an architect and start building.

There are times, though, when it makes sense to buy property late in the game:

1. If you don't own a monopoly.
2. If you own an expensive monopoly that you can't afford to develop, and you have the chance to obtain a cheaper monopoly. For example, if you own Boardwalk, Park Place, St. Charles, and Virginia, it probably makes sense to buy States, sell at least one of the dark-blues, and start building.
3. If you own a monopoly that is fully developed. You may need a second monopoly to deliver the coup de grâce.
4. If your only monopoly is Mediterranean and Baltic, or even the light-blues, and you suspect that's not enough to win the game.
5. If you have a chance to buy a railroad.

That's a long list, but take our word for it: Most players will have no interest in buying property late in the game. They'll be too busy developing their existing monopolies and trying to stay afloat. So most property will be available for the minimum bid. The other players have little choice but to watch you buy.

If someone else is buying property, just grin and bear it. You can try to be clever and bid $115 for New York Avenue after your opponent cavalierly bids $110. But watch out: He may let you have it for $115. You won't feel very clever selling three houses on Virginia to buy a property you don't need.

Up from the Ashes—The Best Ways to Use Bankruptcy

It happens to the best of families. Your million-dollar house burns down, and you're using your steak knives to slice the Spam. You saved for a rainy day, but you just got caught in a hurricane. You're tapped out, broke, ruined.

We can help. In Beyond Boardwalk, the Toppled Tycoon has a Cozy Cushion: bankruptcy. You can turn in your paltry assets—even if you're down to $5—and the Bank will give you

Paradise Lost

$800 plus Mediterranean and Baltic. You may not like those low-rent properties, but at least they'll keep you in the game.

Here are a few ways to use the bankruptcy laws to your advantage:

• *Be sure to be first.* Only one player can declare bankruptcy in each game. Don't let another player beat you to the cash window. If someone else is equally desperate, make sure you declare bankruptcy before he has the chance.

• *Be aware of board position.* The best time to declare bankruptcy is just before you pass Go. That way, your stake will immediately grow from $800 to $1,000. Considering the steep odds against you, you will need every cent.

• *Get ready to gamble.* Even after bankruptcy, you may still be the weakest player in the game. You wouldn't have been in such desperate shape to begin with if there weren't some outrageous rents out there. So you've got to take chances. At the very least, you should immediately build a hotel on Baltic. It costs only $250 and pays rent of $450—a nice return. Mediterranean is a little trickier, since it pays only $250 and is one of the least landed-on properties. But if you don't build on Mediterranean, try something else—fast. Buy property from another player or bid aggressively on unsold property. Pray that you land on Free Parking. To actually *win* the game, you'll need another monopoly—and a lot of luck.

What if you're in good shape when an opponent seems ready to declare bankruptcy? Try buying Baltic or Mediterranean for the minimum bid of $40. The Bank will pay you $120 for each property if another player declares bankruptcy. Also, consider buying property from someone on the verge of bankruptcy. Even if you have to sell it later, at least you will keep it out of the hands of your stronger rivals. And don't worry too much. Bankruptcy gives your opponent a new life, but it is usually brutal and short.

Part Three

Training and Etiquette

Chapter 7

Styles of Play

"Money is better than poverty, if only for financial reasons."

—Woody Allen

Did you ever notice how much games reveal about personality? The showoff who tried a slam dunk from half-court will casually ski backward down the expert slope. The bully who played football like Rambo will play basketball the same way. And the sneak who struck you out with slow curve balls will try to wear you out with drop shots on the tennis court.

In Beyond Boardwalk, we've come across the same personality types. No matter how the game is going, they play it their way. Here are a few specimens:

1. The Skinflint

DESCRIPTION: Offers to drive you to the game, then asks you to pay for the gas. Has a pay phone in his kitchen.

CLOTHING: The sports jacket he wore to his high school prom, twenty-five years ago.

FAVORITE TOKENS: The iron and the thimble (they save money on laundry bills).

FAVORITE CARD: "Bank error in your favor. Collect $200."

TELLTALE SIGNS: Resents the fact that we don't use the $1 bill. Never bids more than the minimum, never makes any trades. Studies your title deed for ten minutes before admitting that he owes you the rent you requested.

HOW TO BEAT HIM: Build, build, build.

2. The Gambler

DESCRIPTION: Never met an auction he didn't like. Uses his last dollar to build a house he doesn't need. Makes side bets on anything from the roll of the dice to the number of bubbles that will rise in his next glass of beer.

CLOTHING: An $800 Armani suit with a custom-made silk shirt.

FAVORITE TOKEN: The sports car.

TELLTALE SIGNS: Arrives late after a long day at the track. Brings his own lucky dice with him. Thinks of Free Parking as "his" square. Plays with *real* cash when he runs out of Monopoly® money.

HOW TO BEAT HIM: Don't do anything. Just let him beat himself.

3. The Loyalty Freak

DESCRIPTION: Loves one color group—usually Boardwalk and Park Place. *Really* loves Boardwalk.

CLOTHING: Same as yesterday. Same as the day before.

The Gambler

TELLTALE SIGNS: Loves to tell you how she beat her older brother by building a hotel on Boardwalk. Doesn't tell you it happened ten years ago. Wonders why Richard Burton didn't give Elizabeth Taylor just one more chance. Watches *Dragnet* reruns instead of *Miami Vice*.

HOW TO BEAT HER: Feed her addiction. If she thinks Boardwalk is worth $600, open the bidding at $610. Your apparent love of "her" property will stir her passion to new heights. Don't worry, you cannot outbid her. And if somehow you do wind up with one of "her" properties, just act smug. Talk about how you beat *your* brother. Pretty soon, the Loyalty Freak will beg for the chance to buy it from you—at double the price you paid.

4. The Rail Baron

DESCRIPTION: Yawns when he lands on Free Parking. Snoozes during the auction for Boardwalk. Wakes up with a start when that first token lands on B & O.

CLOTHING: Engineer's hat, Amtrak tie clip.

FAVORITE TOKEN: A miniature rail car (brings his own).

TELLTALE SIGNS: Has asked you to play every night since you told him Beyond Boardwalk has six railroads. Gives you a ticket when you land on a railroad—even if he doesn't own it.

HOW TO BEAT HIM: Hide the cards that say "Advance token to the nearest Railroad."

5. The Huckster

DESCRIPTION: Talks a great game. Has figured out all the angles. Knows how you can make $1 million in your spare time—guaranteed.

CLOTHING: Flowered Hawaiian shirt and a plaid sports jacket.

FAVORITE TOKEN: Whichever one you're using. Offers to give up his right to the thimble for $50.

TELLTALE SIGNS: Spends $500 to buy Mediterranean Avenue, then proclaims that he's just locked up the game. Goes bankrupt two turns later.

HOW TO BEAT HIM: Bring your earplugs.

6. The Milquetoast

DESCRIPTION: Self-effacing. Doesn't want to offend anyone. He seems happiest when *you* win.

FAVORITE TOKEN: Whichever one you don't want.

TELLTALE SIGNS: Mistakenly moves his token to your hotel on New York instead of Free Parking. Sells you a "Get out of Jail free" card for $5, just to give you a hand.

7. The Artiste

DESCRIPTION: Doesn't like games; agrees to play only because the board is so elegant.

FAVORITE TOKEN: The top hat.

TELLTALE SIGNS: Won't buy the green properties because the color clashes with his sweater. Doesn't mind if his opponents build hotels, as long as they are tastefully designed.

HOW TO BEAT HIM: Ignore him; he doesn't care about winning anyway.

8. The Strong, Silent Type

DESCRIPTION: Mohawk haircut, arms like Arnold Schwarzenegger, legs like Bubba Smith. Makes Dirty Harry look friendly.

FAVORITE TOKEN: The cowboy.

TELLTALE SIGNS: He's a forceful presence, but he keeps his own counsel. Bids selectively, never trades, never smiles. Then, just when you think you've won the game, he builds hotels on the yellows and greens and knocks you out in three turns.

HOW TO BEAT HIM: Are you sure you want to?

Chapter 8

Training for
Beyond Boardwalk
and Park Place

"Genius is one per cent inspiration and ninety-nine per cent perspiration."

—Thomas Edison

Beyond Boardwalk is more than a diversion. It's a fight to the finish, with no quarter asked and none given. It's a world where your friend today will try to break you tomorrow. You cannot walk unprepared into this lonely battle. You must become a lean, mean fighting machine.

After years of research, we have developed a scientific training regimen that will hone your mind and body for the rigors of Beyond Boardwalk. A word of caution: This program is not for everyone. Please consult your doctor before beginning the program or attempting to play.

Basic Training

Although Beyond Boardwalk relies chiefly on mental skills, the game can be physically grueling. You must be ready to endure tense moments at the table, away from family and friends, without the comforts of food, sleep, or your VCR. You

No Guts, No Glory

must be prepared for the full range of the game's physical demands: dealing out money, lifting and rolling the dice, and racing to the refrigerator between turns.

We have found that the following program, if adhered to conscientiously, will allow you to maintain that fine competitive edge:

Monday: Squeeze a tennis ball for ten minutes. Do five pushups—don't strain. By developing your upper body, you will learn to handle even the heaviest dice with ease.

Tuesday: Run two miles. Swim one-half mile. Ride a bicycle for five minutes. Easy does it.

Wednesday: Run ten miles. Breathe deeply for five minutes. Run ten more. This will prepare you for that long trek to the refrigerator.

Thursday: Bench press 400 pounds. SAFETY FIRST—be sure to use a spotter.

Friday: Swim the English Channel. Be sure to take the Concorde—you'll want to be well rested before your swim. Also, you have a tough day tomorrow.

Saturday: Climb Mount Everest. Remember: Endurance counts.

Sunday: Game time. Beyond Boardwalk begins at seven P.M., after the NFL doubleheader.

Please note: Because this is a demanding program, we do not recommend that you follow it every week. Some weeks, you may want to give yourself a breather. For example, on the second Monday we generally cut back to only three pushups.

Eating Well

Doctors at the Beyond Boardwalk and Park Place Foundation have made a remarkable discovery: If you like something, it must be good for you. The Beyond Boardwalk diet allows you to eat the food you enjoy, without feeling guilty. Just choose liberally from among the four basic food groups:

1. Malt beverages. Includes beer, ale, and lager. Most nutritious when consumed in sixteen-ounce "tall boy" cans. Warning: Do not accept "light" beers. Beyond Boardwalk is not for lightweights.
2. Chocolate. Includes Ring Dings, Yodels, Ice Cubes, Mr. Goodbar, Yoo-hoo, and chocolate chocolate-chip ice cream. Does *not* include: chocolate/vanilla/strawberry ice cream served in one container, carob, or Tofutti.
3. Other sugared products. Recommended: candy corn, Cap'n Crunch, Twinkies, glazed doughnuts, and Mister Softee ice cream.
4. Grease and salt. Includes beef jerky, barbecue potato chips, Cheez Doodles, and fried pork rinds.

Caution: Do not eat anything that grows on trees. It may be contaminated by Alar, DDT, or other pesticides. For any product in the four basic food groups, colorful plastic packaging is your best guarantee of quality.

Mental Training

Exercise and diet are great, but they are not enough. Beyond Boardwalk requires discipline, concentration, and an unbending will to win. It's this kind of mental toughness that separates the magnates from the milquetoasts. And toughness is developed through the habits of a lifetime; there are no shortcuts.

At least not until now. For a limited time only, the Beyond Boardwalk Foundation is offering master classes in the mental skills needed to win. To see if you qualify, try completing this simple test:

1. Read an entire issue of *U.S. News & World Report*. Don't forget the "Business Briefing."
2. Try eating just one Lay's potato chip.
3. Name every host who has appeared on the *CBS Morning News*.*
4. Sit through an entire speech by Walter Mondale. No yawning.
5. Spend an hour with Howard Cosell.
6. Explain the tie-breaker system for determining which teams get into the NFL play-offs. Then explain why they don't just flip a coin.
7. Tell your kids they can't watch *The A Team*. Make it stick.
8. Explain your decision to Mr. T.

Give yourself 10 points for every completed task.

If you scored fewer than 60 points, you're welcome to join our game any time. With a little pressure, you're the kind of person who would trade us Baltic Avenue for Marvin Gardens, straight up. People like you are hard to find.

If you scored 60 or 70, you are a dangerous opponent. We'd spend a few hours polishing our excuses before we tangled with you.

If you scored 80, you are permanently barred from Beyond Boardwalk championship play. People like you are always getting in our way. Have you ever considered enlisting in the Green Berets?

If you scored 90 or more, count again, Jack. The maximum score is 80. And pardon us for being blunt, but you remind us of that crooked Banker in the game we supposedly lost last week. . . .

---

*Extra credit if you remember Sally Quinn

Chapter 9

Sportsmanship

"For when the one Great Scorer comes,
To write against your name,
He marks—not that you won or lost—
But how you played the game."
—Grantland Rice

One of the most important parts of Beyond Boardwalk is good sportsmanship. We don't mean that sissy stuff about concern for the less fortunate, or helping a friend when he's down. Leave that for the Boy Scouts. The meek may inherit the earth, but you don't have time to wait. So here are a few tips:

Sportsmanship 101: Starting the Game

• *Don't forget to forget names.* If you're playing with people you've never met before, don't make the mistake of getting too friendly before the game. To avoid those complicated personal ties, make it a point to forget names. Better yet, don't listen the first time. Step out for a drink just as the introductions are being made. Remember: It's easier to fleece a stranger than a friend.

• *Don't explain all the rules.* When you've read this book, you will know how to play. Your opponent won't. This is a big advantage—don't give it up lightly. Explain the rules on a need-to-know basis. No point in confusing your opponent with too much information in the beginning. There will be plenty of time to elaborate later on. For example, a good time to explain the Jail rule is when your opponent is in Jail, and you land on Boardwalk.

Sportsmanship 102: If You're Winning

• *Show concern for your opponent.* Suppose you're rich but your opponent is down on his luck. You land on a railroad and bid $110. Your opponent, crestfallen, says he'll have to pass. Don't let this moment slide. Remind him that you already have four railroads. Point out that earlier in the game, he bid $350 for B & O, and ask him if he's changed his views. Your opponent may act annoyed, but deep down he'll be grateful that you're looking out for his interests.

• *Provide some historical perspective.* Suppose you own a hotel on New York Avenue and your opponent lands on it. The Boy Scout would ask politely for his $1,000 and leave it at that. Don't be so thoughtless. Your opponent may be wondering where he went wrong. Take the time to explain it. After all, those who ignore history are condemned to repeat it.

• *Don't wait for a special occasion.* The amateur sportsman will save his helpful remarks for those moments when his opponent is particularly helpless. The professional knows that good advice is always timely. So don't wait until you have a decisive advantage—that happy moment may never come. Speak up any time there's a lull in the conversation. Or just interrupt if one of your opponents is saying something dull.

Sportsmanship 103: If You're Losing

• *This is no time for laughs*. A lot of people think it's okay to make jokes or exchange pleasantries during the game. That's fine—if *you* happen to be winning. If you're losing, though, it's no laughing matter. Let everyone know that you can't stand small talk. Make it clear that for you, the game comes first.

• *It's all luck anyway*. Your opponent may think he's winning because of superior skill. Don't let him labor under this delusion. Point out that everything depends on the roll of the dice. Tell him that your high school football team could beat the Chicago Bears if it got as lucky as he did. This may seem harsh, but if you care about your opponent, you won't want him to get a swelled head.

• *Try guerrilla tactics*. Sometimes your friends will ignore your warnings and continue to enjoy their good fortune. This is the time to take action. Try grabbing a little extra cash from the Bank—or maybe a property card nobody has spotted. Overcharge someone who's rich. If all else fails, tip the board over and announce that it's time for a new game.

Chapter 10
The All-Purpose
Excuse Guide

"A bad excuse is better than none."
—Sixteenth-century proverb

With this book you should be able to win more often than not. But eventually it happens to everyone—you're bound to lose a game. And while we may not be able to save you from a beating, we won't leave you speechless.

Some people would just shake hands and say, "Nice game." But nobody likes a hypocrite. And deep in your heart you know that you deserved to win. So in the interest of candor, here are a few explanations as to why justice did not prevail:

1. Weather: Just because you played inside doesn't mean you liked the weather. It may have been too hot, too cold, too drafty, too stuffy, too humid, too anything. Just don't complain about the rain.
2. Luck: No matter how badly you played, you can always blame your bad luck. Even if you landed on Free Parking every time around the board, there was some roll, sometime, that didn't go your way. Discuss it—at length.
3. Distractions: The kids were screaming. You hated the wallpaper. There was too much traffic noise. Any excuse will do. The point is: Your mind was on anything

but the game. The implication is: If you hadn't been so distracted, you would have won easily.

4. Injuries: Every time you rolled the dice, your wrist locked up on you. You stopped bidding because you had a sore throat. The guacamole dip gave you a stomachache. Sure you lost, but it's a miracle that you could play at all.

5. Fatigue: You were up all night closing that million-dollar deal. You had a heavy date and got only two hours of sleep. Or you slept until noon and were still drowsy when the game began.

6. You let the other guy win: You're such a nice guy, you like to spread the glory around. Where's the fun if one person wins every time?

7. What's the big deal?—It's only a game. (Use this one sparingly, and preferably with strangers. Even if you rehearse it, your friends will never believe you.)

Atlantic City—Then and Now

"The gambling known as business looks with austere disfavor on the business known as gambling."
 —Ambrose Bierce

Atlantic City was founded in 1854, when Richard Osborne built a railroad line out to Absecon Island, just off the coast of southern New Jersey. Osborne created a "Bathing Village" which he hoped would serve as the "lungs of Philadelphia." The city is located on the northern part of Absecon Island, and is roughly fifty-five miles southeast of Philadelphia.

Atlantic City flourished in the 1920s and 1930s, mostly because it was so accessible to New York and Philadelphia. The city had airs of exclusivity, but it was never really a favorite of the carriage trade. For all the glitter and gangsters, it was a down-to-earth, middle-class resort. The Miss America pageant, hucksterish but wholesome, was an apt symbol for the city.

This was the Atlantic City commemorated on Charles Darrow's Depression-era board. The east-west streets are named after the seas, and the north-south streets after the states. In the city, and on the Monopoly® board, everything was orderly, comfortable, neat.

Times have changed. Since 1978, Atlantic City has been transformed by casinos—first Resorts International, and then Caesars and Golden Nugget and the other big names in gam-

bling. Now there's a whole strip of casinos, glistening and gar-
ish, towering over the Boardwalk. They offer luxury suites and
sumptuous meals, championship boxing and big-name enter-
tainment. And, of course, gambling. Atlantic City may be eco-
nomically depressed, but the casinos are booming.

Atlantic City has said goodbye to the Horatio Alger virtues
of thrift and discipline and hard work. The city has become a
crapshoot. Make a fortune in one night—and lose it in one
hour. It's a place for high rollers, feeding off the action. It's not
like the old Atlantic City.

And so it seemed time for a new approach to Monopoly®,
the game built on the virtues of the old Atlantic City. Time to
put some risk into the game, and some excitement. Time to
have players bidding against each other, thumbing their noses
at the humorless Bank, living on the edge. Time to move beyond Boardwalk, into the world of high stakes and high fi-
nance.

So if you like to gamble, you'll probably like Beyond
Boardwalk. And if you don't, why not try it anyway? Because
Beyond Boardwalk, in the end, is far more forgiving than those
imposing casinos. When your money runs short, when some
tycoon knocks you out of the game, you're not really hurled
into the poorhouse. After all, it's only play money. Just shuffle
the *Go* cards and start a new game.

Appendices

Appendix A

For Addicts Only

If you've read this far, you know our rules inside and out, and you have a good idea of how to apply them. This section is designed to back up some of our casual observations with hard data.

Instant Bankruptcy

Players with a taste for offbeat strategies should consider declaring bankruptcy on their first turn. Instead of starting the game with $1,500 and no property, you start with $800, plus the Mediterranean/Baltic monopoly. If you invest $250 to build a hotel on Baltic, you have a chance to earn $450 in rent before the other players even buy their first property.

Instant bankruptcy works best if you are lucky enough to go first. This means that you can build your hotel while everyone else is still on Go. Since the other players are just three squares away from Baltic Avenue, there is a chance that someone will visit your hotel on his first turn.

This strategy is a long shot in a three- or four-player game, but with five or six players it may be worth trying. Assuming that you roll first, in a three-player game there is an 11 percent chance that at least one of the other two players will land on Baltic on his first turn. In a four-player game, the probability is 16 percent; in a five-player game, 20 percent; and in a six-player game, 25 percent.

If someone does land, you're in great shape. You will have

$1,000 in cash ($800 from bankruptcy, less $250 for a hotel, plus $450 in rent), plus Mediterranean and Baltic, plus a hotel on Baltic. But until someone lands, you will have significantly less cash than the other players, and it will be hard for you to buy property.

A Few Words About Jail

In compiling the probability chart (see pages 25-26), Professor Hentzel assumed that players would stay In Jail as long as possible (i.e., either three turns or until they threw doubles). His probabilities for Jail and Just Visiting are as follows:

Sent to Jail	.0444
Been In Jail one turn	.0370
Been In Jail two turns	.0308
Just Visiting	.0254
TOTAL	.1376

In Beyond Boardwalk, players who are In Jail cannot bid on property, cannot build, and collect only half the usual rent. As a result, players usually get out of Jail immediately, and the percentages for "Been In Jail one turn" and "Been In Jail two turns" are much, much lower. But even if everyone got out of Jail immediately, the Jail/Just Visiting square would still be the square landed on most frequently:

Sent to Jail	.0444
Just Visiting	.0254
TOTAL	.0698

This means that there is at least a 6.98 percent chance of landing on this square, which is roughly double the chance of landing on Illinois Avenue (3.55 percent), the next most-visited square.

Earnings Per Turn

Which properties are likely to earn the most money? The concept of "earnings per turn" helps answer that question. Earnings per turn considers both the amount of rent you can charge if somebody lands on your property, and the likelihood that someone will land (for the landing probabilities, see pages 25-26). For example, if you have one house on Connecticut Avenue, you can charge your opponent $40 each time he lands. Since he will land on Connecticut roughly once every forty turns (the landing probability is actually .0257), you can expect to earn, on average, about $1 (or more precisely, $1.03) from Connecticut each time your opponent picks up the dice.

The following table is based on the landing probabilities developed by Professor Irvin Hentzel. The concept of "earnings per turn" was introduced by Dr. Crypton, with the aid of Stephen Heppe of Stanford Telecommunications Inc., in an article published in the September 1985 issue of *Science Digest*.

EARNINGS PER TURN (FOR PROPERTIES IN COLOR GROUPS)

PROPERTY	REVENUE PER TURN				
	If you own				
	1 house	2 houses	3 houses	4 houses	hotel
Mediterranean	$0.24	$ 0.71	$ 2.14	$ 3.81	$ 5.96
Baltic	0.48	1.45	4.35	7.74	10.88
Oriental	0.75	2.27	6.83	10.12	13.92
Vermont	0.78	2.34	7.01	10.38	14.28
Connecticut	1.03	2.57	7.72	11.58	15.44
St. Charles	1.52	4.55	13.65	18.96	22.75
States	1.29	3.87	11.61	16.13	19.35
Virginia	1.73	5.18	14.39	20.15	25.91
St. James	2.23	6.36	17.50	23.86	30.22
Tennessee	2.34	6.70	18.41	25.11	31.81
New York	2.67	7.34	20.02	26.70	33.37

Kentucky	2.79	7.76	21.72	27.15	32.58
Indiana	2.74	7.62	21.32	26.66	31.99
Illinois	3.55	10.65	26.64	32.86	39.08
Atlantic	3.31	9.94	24.09	29.36	34.63
Ventnor	3.29	9.87	23.92	29.15	34.38
Marvin Gardens	3.47	10.42	24.60	29.66	34.73
Pacific	3.89	11.68	26.96	32.95	38.19
North Carolina	3.81	11.44	26.41	32.28	37.41
Pennsylvania	4.19	12.57	27.93	33.51	39.10
Park Place	4.28	12.22	26.89	31.78	36.67
Boardwalk	5.89	17.68	41.26	50.10	58.94

EARNINGS PER TURN (FOR RAILROADS)

RAILROAD   **REVENUE PER TURN**

| | If you own | | | | | |
RAILROAD	1 RR	2 RR	3 RR	4 RR	5 RR	6 RR
Reading	$0.83	$1.62	$3.32	$6.65	$9.97	$13.30
Electric Company	0.78	1.55	3.10	6.21	9.31	12.41
Pennsylvania	0.78	1.56	3.13	6.26	9.38	12.51
B & O	0.86	1.72	3.43	6.86	10.30	13.73
Water Works	0.79	1.57	3.15	6.29	9.44	12.58
Short Line	0.68	1.36	2.72	5.44	8.16	10.87

Earnings Per Turn Per Investment

How many houses should you build to earn the best return? Where should you build them? Some answers can be found in the following table. For each property, the table shows the earnings per turn for each dollar invested in housing. For example, Mediterranean Avenue with one house (cost: $50) earns just half a cent per turn for each dollar invested in housing. As a result, it will take two hundred turns (roughly forever) to earn back your investment. With a hotel, you do much better—2.4 cents per turn per housing dollar—but that is still nothing to write home about.

By contrast, Boardwalk with three houses earns almost 7

cents each turn (actually 6.9 cents) for each dollar invested in housing. You can expect to earn back your investment in only fifteen turns.

Property	1 house	2 houses	3 houses	4 houses	hotel
Mediterranean	$0.005	$0.007	$0.014	$0.019	$0.024
Baltic	0.010	0.015	0.029	0.039	0.044
Oriental	0.015	0.023	0.045	0.051	0.056
Vermont	0.016	0.023	0.047	0.052	0.057
Connecticut	0.021	0.026	0.051	0.058	0.062
St. Charles	0.015	0.023	0.046	0.047	0.046
States	0.013	* 0.019	0.039	0.040	0.039
Virginia	0.017	0.026	0.048	0.050	0.052
St. James	0.022	0.032	0.058	0.060	0.060
Tennessee	0.023	0.034	0.061	0.063	0.064
New York	0.027	0.037	0.067	0.067	0.067
Kentucky	0.019	0.026	0.048	0.045	0.043
Indiana	0.018	0.025	0.047	0.044	0.043
Illinois	0.024	0.036	0.059	0.055	0.052
Atlantic	0.022	0.033	0.054	0.049	0.046
Ventnor	0.022	0.033	0.053	0.049	0.046
Marvin Gardens	0.023	0.035	0.055	0.049	0.046
Pacific	0.019	0.029	0.045	0.041	0.038
North Carolina	0.019	0.029	0.044	0.040	0.037
Pennsylvania	0.021	0.031	0.046	0.042	0.039
Park Place	0.021	0.031	0.045	0.040	0.037
Boardwalk	0.029	0.044	0.069	0.063	0.059

Which One Does Not Belong?

The Monopoly® board is based on the streets of Atlantic City, but one property does not really belong on the board. Marven Gardens is actually four miles southwest of Atlantic City, between the towns of Margate and Ventnor. And the proper spelling is "Marven"—not "Marvin," as it is spelled on the board.

Short Line is not really a railroad at all, but a bus company serving New York and New Jersey. So our decision to convert Water Works and Electric Company into railroads is in keeping with the tradition of the game.

The Official Rules of Beyond Boardwalk and Park Place

1. BUYING PROPERTY: Landing on a property gives a player the right to buy it at double the list price. For example, if a player lands on New York Avenue, which has a list price of $200, he may buy it for $400. The option to buy exists only for the player who lands on a property, and only on his opening bid.

2. AUCTIONING PROPERTY: If the player decides not to buy at double the list price, he may begin the auction. The minimum bid is 50 percent of the list price, plus $10. For example, the minimum bid for New York Avenue (list price $200) is $110.

    If the player who lands on the property does not want to make the first bid, he may pass. Then, moving clockwise, each player in turn has the right to make an opening bid. If every player passes on the opening round, the property remains unsold, and it becomes available again the next time someone lands on it. Otherwise, the bidding continues until one player has made a bid that the remaining players, bidding in order, choose not to top. Each new bid must be at least $5 higher than the previous high bid.

3. THE WINNING BID: The player who wins the auction must immediately pay the Bank the full amount of his bid. If he does not have enough cash on hand, he may attempt to raise money by selling other property or by making a trade. If the player is still unable to pay the Bank, he is involuntarily bankrupt, and loses the game.

4. RESALE OF PROPERTY: A player may sell any property back to the Bank at any time, for one half its list price. For example, a player may sell New York Avenue back to the Bank for $100. However, a property may *not* be mortgaged. You cannot borrow money from the Bank under any circumstances.

5. THE RAILROADS: The utilities (Water Works and Electric Company) are treated like railroads. In Monopoly®, the list price for Water Works and Electric Company is $150. In Beyond Boardwalk, the "list price" is $200, the initial bid is $110, and the resale price—if the property is sold to the Bank—is $100. The rent for the six railroads (Reading, Pennsylvania, B & O, Short Line, Electric Company, and Water Works) is as follows:

If you own 1 railroad	$ 25
If you own 2 railroads	$ 50
If you own 3 railroads	$100
If you own 4 railroads	$200
If you own 5 railroads	$300
If you own 6 railroads	$400

6. UNEVEN BUILDING: A player who owns a monopoly does not have to build evenly on each of his properties. You may build houses in any order you choose, as long as you own the monopoly. For example, if you own St. James Avenue, Tennessee Avenue, and New York Avenue, you are entitled to place four houses or a hotel on New York Avenue even if you have no houses on either St. James or Tennessee.

7. WHEN YOU CAN BUILD: You can only buy houses or hotels immediately before the beginning of your turn.

8. JAIL: If you are in Jail, you may not bid on property, you may not build houses, and you collect only half the rent to which you would normally be entitled. For example, if you own

St. Charles Place (rent: $10), and someone lands on St. Charles while you are in Jail, you are entitled to collect only $5. You may, however, pay to get out of Jail (or use a "Get Out of Jail Free" card) immediately before the turn of any player, at which point you move your token from in Jail to Just Visiting. Players in Jail are still entitled to make trades with other players.

9. SINGLES BARRED: The $1 bills are not used. All rents are rounded off to the next highest $5. For example, the rent on North Carolina Avenue (list rent $26) is $30. The rent on North Carolina if you hold the green monopoly (two times $26, or $52) is $55.

10. GO CARDS: Any player who lands on Go collects $200 and draws a Go card. He must follow the instructions on the card. (A complete set of Go cards is included at the end of this book.)

11. CHAPTER 11: If a player is not in debt to the Bank or to any other player, he may declare voluntary bankruptcy. Upon declaring bankruptcy, he must surrender all of his property, houses, money, "Get Out of Jail Free" cards, and Go cards to the Bank. The Bank then pays him $800 and gives him the title deeds for Mediterranean Avenue and Baltic Avenue. If another player owns Mediterranean Avenue and/or Baltic Avenue, the Bank pays that player $120 for each property being repossessed. If either property has been developed, the Bank repossesses the houses and pays the owner $50 for each house. If a player is in debt to the Bank or to another player, he may not declare bankruptcy until he pays his debt. If he is unable to pay his debt, he is involuntarily bankrupt, and he loses the game. Voluntary bankruptcy can be used only once in each game. After one player declares voluntary bankruptcy, no other player may do so in that game.

12. ADVANCE TO NEAREST RAILROAD OR UTILITY: If a player draws the *Chance* card saying "Advance token to the nearest Railroad. . ." he must advance to either Reading Railroad, Pennsylvania Railroad, or B & O Railroad, whichever is the nearest, and follow the instructions on the card. (Short Line is never the nearest railroad, since there is no Chance square between B & O and Short Line). If a player draws the *Chance* card saying "Advance token to nearest utility . . ." he must advance to either Electric Company or Water Works, whichever is nearer. After moving his token, the player must disregard the instructions printed on the card. Instead, he must pay the owner *twice* the rent to which the owner would otherwise be entitled. If the utility is unowned, he may buy it for $400, open the bidding (minimum bid $110), or pass.

13. FREE PARKING: All fines, taxes, and house assessments are paid into a kitty, which is kept in the middle of the board, rather than to the Bank. If a player lands on Free Parking, he collects all the money (if any) in the kitty.

14. INCOME TAX: If a player lands on Income Tax, he may calculate the value of his assets (cash, property, houses, and hotels) before deciding whether he should pay $200 or 10 percent of the value of his assets.

Appendix C

Variations

Developing the rules for Beyond Boardwalk and Park Place was a process of trial and error. We started with a few goals: to put more skill, more risk, and more excitement into the game. We experimented with dozens of rules that seemed to promote those goals. Some had loopholes that we tried to close. Others affected the game in ways we hadn't anticipated. For example, when we tried giving bankrupt players $1,000, instead of $800, we found that many players were declaring bankruptcy before their first turn. Other rules made sense to us, but not to anyone else. And we had to reject a few rules for a very practical reason: They were too complicated. We wanted to make sure that explaining the rules took less time than playing the game.

The rules we liked best became the official rules of Beyond Boardwalk and Park Place. But a few variations work well enough that we'd like to pass them on:

1. BUILDING WITHOUT A MONOPOLY: Players can build houses or hotels on their property even if they don't own a monopoly. But they must pay a stiff price for the privilege. First, before building on any property, they must pay $100 into Free Parking to obtain a "building permit." Second, houses cost twice the list price. For example, to build on New York Avenue without owning Tennessee Avenue and St. James Place as well, you must pay $200 for each house, instead of the $100 it would cost if you had the monopoly. If you resell houses to the Bank, the Bank pays you the usual resale price—that is, half the list price

of the house. Therefore, if you resell a house on New York Avenue, the Bank pays you only $50.

2. BUYING WITHOUT LANDING: Each player has the right, one time in each game, to buy unowned property directly from the Bank, even if nobody has landed on the property. The price for this special purchase is three times the list price. This means that if you desperately need Oriental Avenue (list price $100) to complete a monopoly, you can buy it from the Bank for $300.

3. MORTGAGE INTEREST: In this version, we restore the practice of mortgaging property—but with a twist. Every time you pass Go, you must pay 10 percent interest on all your outstanding debt. If you have mortgaged Boardwalk (mortgage value $200), you must pay the Bank $20 every time you pass Go with Boardwalk still mortgaged.

4. BANKRUPTCY VARIATIONS: Making a bankruptcy rule is a balancing act. We've tried to give the voluntarily bankrupt player enough money to afford him an outside chance to win. The official rules say that a bankrupt player receives $800, in addition to Mediterranean and Baltic Avenues. We have found, though, that $800 may be too little money in a three-player game, and too much in a six-player game. The rules can provide for a different bankruptcy stake depending on the number of players left in the game:

Number of players still in the game (including the bankrupt player)	Bankrupt player receives
3	$950
4	$850
5	$750
6	$700

5. ROBBER BARON—THE LIBERTARIAN VERSION OF BEYOND BOARDWALK: Robber Baron is a set of rules designed to put maximum skill into the game. These rules give you total free-

dom to build and trade whenever and however you please. We find this game challenging, but also a bit slow. Players sometimes spend so much time making deals that the game loses some of its action and spontaneity. But for expert players, this is an interesting variation. Here's how Robber Baron works:

A. You can build houses after any roll of the dice, even in the middle of another player's turn.
B. You can make trades during an auction.
C. You can make trades that affect your right to bid.
D. There is no minimum bid in the auction. You can bid $5 for Boardwalk, and if the other players are desperately poor, you may get it.

6. GOING TO JAIL—VOLUNTARILY: This variation gives each player one reprieve from the whimsy of the dice. Once each game, you are allowed to skip a turn. Instead of rolling the dice, you surrender to the sheriff and proceed directly to Jail. This gives you an escape hatch at that awful moment when you just *know* you're about to land on your opponent's hotel.

The Do-It-Yourself
Go Card Kit

The *Go* cards printed on the next few pages are all the new equipment you need for Beyond Boardwalk. To use them, just cut along the dotted lines, stack the cards in the middle of the board (we usually place them near the Go To Jail square), and select the top card whenever you land on Go.

Please note that these "cards" are printed on regular paper; they won't stand up to heavy use. If you are concerned about wear and tear, glue these pages to some cardboard before you cut out the cards.

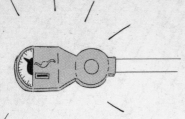

ADVANCE
TO FREE PARKING
and collect the
jackpot, if any.
Give $50 to each player
as a tip for
parking your car.

YOUR FRIENDS
HONOR YOU AS
"TYCOON OF THE
YEAR."
Collect $50 from
each player.

THE CITY CONDEMNS
ONE OF YOUR HOUSES.
Sell one house
back to the
Bank at ½ the
price you paid for it.

YOU HOLD A PARTY
to curry favor with
community leaders.
Pay $25 for the curry.

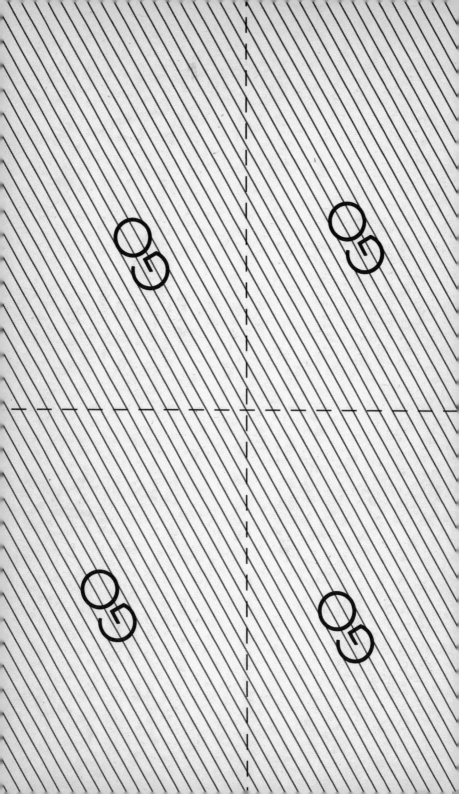

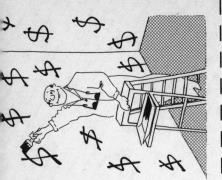

YOUR RENOVATIONS
PAY OFF.
Collect $50 extra
rent from the next
player who lands
on any of your
properties.

THE RAILROADS
RUN LATE—AGAIN.
If you own
any railroads,
pay each player $50
as a refund
for poor service.

You win a
"NIGHT ON THE
HOUSE."
The next time
you land on anyone
else's property,
you are excused
from paying rent.

YOU DECIDE
TO TAKE UP GOLF.
Pay each
player $25 for
private lessons.

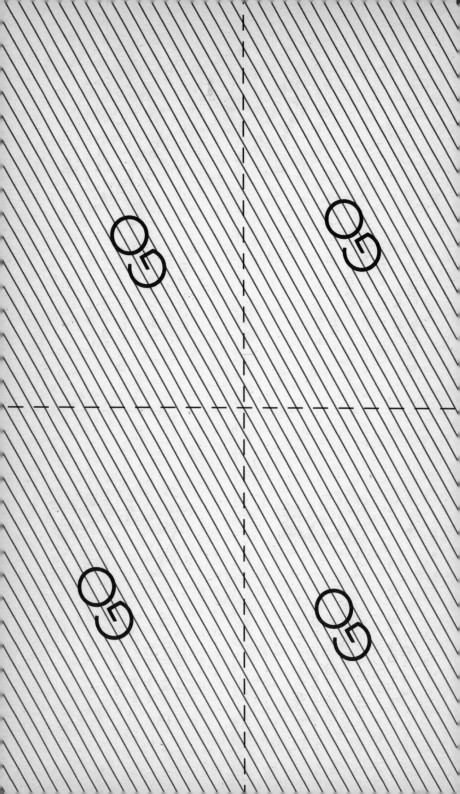

The railroads
announce a
SPECIAL YOUTH FARE.
Deduct 50% from
the rent the next
time you land
on someone else's
railroad.

YOU'VE BEEN
ELECTED SHERIFF.
Send another
player to jail.

Your brother-in-law
becomes
PRESIDENT OF THE
BANK.
The Bank will
contribute $100 to
your final bid
in the next auction.

YOU MARRY
ONE OF YOUR TENANTS.
Collect $25 from
each player as
a wedding gift.

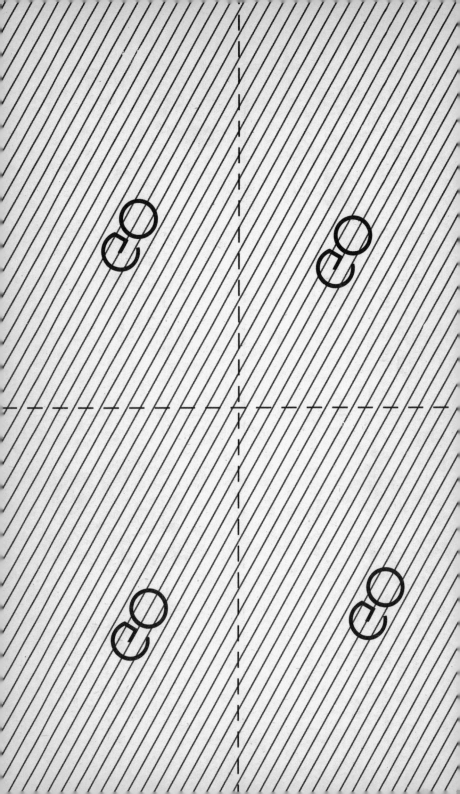

The Beyond Boardwalk and Park Place Association

The Beyond Boardwalk and Park Place Association has been organized to promote Beyond Boardwalk and Park Place, refine the rules, develop strategy, and encourage tournament play. While Monopoly® has restricted its marketing efforts to only thirty-two countries, we welcome members from all over the globe. If you would like to join, if you have any comments about the rules or strategy, or if you'd just like to tell us about an interesting game you played, please write to:

The Beyond Boardwalk and Park Place Association
P.O. Box 18343
Washington, D.C. 20036

ABOUT THE AUTHORS

Noel Gunther and Richard Hutton are longtime friends and Monopoly® rivals.

Between games, Noel Gunther works as a lawyer and freelance writer in Washington, D.C. He has written for *The Village Voice*, *Washingtonion*, *Washington Journalism Review*, and *Adweek*. Noel is a graduate of Yale University and Harvard Law School.

Richard Hutton has written eight books on science and medicine. Most recently, he developed and co-produced the award-winning PBS series *The Brain*. He commutes regularly from New York to Washington for his Beyond Boardwalk fix.